CROW CALL

Crow Call

Poems by Michael Henson

WEST END PRESS

Poems from *Crow Call* have been published in *Appalachian Connection*, *Blue Collar Review*, *The Cincinnati Review*, *The Merton Seasonal*, *Out of Line*, *Pemmican*, *Pine Mountain Sand & Gravel*, *Red Crow Poetry Journal*, *Threepenny Review*, and in the anthology *Smaller than God: Words of Spiritual Longing* (Black Moss Press). A selection of these poems won the 2002 Jack Kerouac Poetry Prize. Nearly all have run in *StreetVibes*, the newspaper of the Greater Cincinnati Coalition for the Homeless.

First edition, November 2006
ISBN: 0-9753486-6-3   (978-0-9753486-6-6)

Book and cover design by Nancy Woodard
Cover photograph by Amanda Gardner
Author photograph by Jimmy Heath

West End Press • P.O. Box 27334 • Albuquerque, NM 87125

Contents

Author's Note

These are poems created in response to the death of a friend, buddy gray. None of the poems mention him by name; some do not mention him at all. But each of these poems arose, in the way of poems, out of the emotional and political consequences of his death. gray (he preferred his name in lower case) was a Cincinnati activist, a co-founder of the National Coalition for the Homeless, and the director of a local homeless shelter. He was a relentless and uncompromising advocate for low-income housing and other services for the poor; he earned, thereby, the respect and love of many. He also earned the remarkably bitter hatred of some developers and some politicians, including, of course, some developer-politicians. For months before his death, an unknown person (or persons, or class of persons) maintained a campaign which featured death threats, stop-sign-shaped stickers reading "STOP BUDDY GRAY," and, if you dialed a certain number, a seven-minute, anti-buddy recorded message. On November 15, 1996, a mentally ill, formerly homeless man buddy had befriended shot and killed buddy in his office. No one knows if the man had contacts with the STOP-BUDDY-GRAY campaign. No one knows how he obtained the expensive pistol he used in the shooting. The man was declared unfit to stand trial and remains in a hospital. Within an hour of buddy's death, the phone recording was disconnected.

Eight days later, over two thousand people from Cincinnati, Boston, Washington, Chicago, and other cities marched silently through the streets in honor of buddy gray and in support of the homeless.

Comerado, I give you my hand!
I give you my love
more precious than money,
I give you myself
before preaching or law;
Will you give me yourself?
Will you come travel with me?
Shall we stick by each other
as long as we live?

Whitman
"Song of the Open Road"

Let Love clasp grief lest both be drowned
Let darkness keep her raven gloss

Tennyson
"In Memoriam"

Invocation

There is a thing I want to say,
but I think my voice is much too small.
I fear my voice will never answer to what I need it now to do.
Too much, my brothers
Too much, my sisters.
Today I feel it is just too much
and my small voice, my thin and compromised voice,
will not answer to what is needed.
I have come up out of the corn
and into this forest of concrete and obfuscation
and I have a thing to say.
But the liar is cozy and respected
and he beams from a thousand channels.
He has a voice of rushing megahertz
he is marble-footed and leatherbound
he has a senatorial larynx
he is a citadel of sincerity
and speaks with the long slick tongue of television.
Even when we sleep, he comes to us in a whisper of silicon.
He slides down the invisible paths of the fiber optic.
Even in our dreams
he is woofing and tweeting and coughing and farting
fouling the air with the smell of money and fear.
But the true word is still true.
It is not hard to tell it or to speak it.
It only takes a simple human voice.
But when our voices are so small. . . .
A child, mumbling among the trousered pillars of a room,
a bird, trilling and cheeping in the nettles,
a curse lost in the rattle of the factory,
the wheeze of the asthmatic,
a rabbit with his single *speak* in the claws of a hawk—
they have such small voices.
My own voice is thin as a reed.
My throat,
with which I was voiced by my father,
is no thicker than a stalk of corn
and I think it is much too small.

My voice is two dimes in a pocket.
My voice is a little, pecked-over crust of bread.
My voice is a letter, mailed long ago and shut up in a box.
My voice is the distant call of a crow.
My voice is a little black net of smoke.
My voice is a dry grass that makes the sound
of a little dry shaking in the wind.

But I have a little trick
and I will use it.
I hold myself close to the earth,
close enough to hear the hidden engineering of the ants,
close enough to hear
the yearning and absorption of the roots.
I fix myself in the smell of cinder and vegetation
where bone becomes stem
and leaf, moldering,
exhales its little wisp of methane
where the centipede trickles over the composted bark
where the mole digs his shallow mine.
There, I call upon the ancestors,
on Debs and Tubman, King and Neruda
Whitman, Lorca, and Florence Reece.
Tom McGrath and Joe Hill, I call
William Blake and Aunt Molly Jackson.
I spread wide my chest.
I fill my lungs with moldered rags,
root hairs
broken glass
and the earthen voices of the dead
        and I speak.

BOOK I

Witness

Keen of sirens,
flash of blue lights, flash of red.
A murmur of voices in the street:
Curious, a pair of crows
circles in the cold morning air.
There is neither food nor danger here,
so they alight at the base of a steeple to watch.
Below, the human crowd mills and ponders.
Some rush in and out at a door.
Some give orders.
Some stalk the street,
each with a great black eye at his shoulder.
Some merely shiver in the cold and,
like these two birds, watch.
Minutes pass, a gurney rolls from out the door
and is swallowed by a white truck
as a shad is swallowed by a bass.
Again the sirens! Faster the lights!
The white bass of the ambulance
bears the gurney away.
More minutes,
a bound man is forced out into the street.
He struggles, he curses.
The two men who bind him are grim as serpents.
They stuff him down the maw of a white car
and shut the door.
Again the sirens, the milling lights.
The one-eyed ones
take down the eyes from their shoulders
and are men again
and are gone in cars.
The ones who remain in the cold
talk in small groups among themselves.
Some quietly, others in loud, sharp tones.
They gesture with hard, argumentative cuts with their hands.

The two crows in the steeple
ruff their feathers for warmth.
They will watch for some time more.
Then at dusk
will take what they have gathered
to their cold roosts in the hillside.

Poem of the Gurney

So is this the end of our old argument?

I never thought to see you lie so still.
Nor so quiet!
Strange, to see you here,
and naked,
in that little antiseptic chapel of a room,
under that sheet,
with such a chest swelling the sheet
and such shoulders
rolling out from under that sheet
and all that hair
spread out across the head of the gurney.
And your face!
Brother, why was your face so gray?
And why the blue-gray bruises
swelling under your eyes?

My mother dwindled before she died.
She had all the spindling weight of a leaf.
She was two puffs of air
and a set of tied-up bones
and a night gown.
Then she was just one puff of air.
Then she was nothing at all.

But just yesterday,
just yesterday,
you had a broad breathing set of lungs
and a steady beating heart
and a chest strong as beef
and shoulders round and thick.
You had balls and beard and sweat
and a twist of intestines
for grinding up those godawful day-old sandwiches.

And now, my brother,
who nailed you to this gurney?

And why is your face the color of ash?

Song of the Crows

It once was rare to see a crow in the city.
Crows were country birds, shy of humans.
If you came on a group of them in a field,
they would lift, flappety-flap!
like a dismembered black blanket
cawing and croaking in a dozen voices:
Invasion! invasion! a warning!
Now, they have come to the city.
No one knows why
or what they find here.
In the day, I see them
singly, and in pairs
pecking at the eye of a roadkill squirrel
sampling a castoff potato chip
or snapping at the heads of the grasses
in an empty lot.
They are everywhere,
common as pigeon or sparrow.
At sundown, they gather in the hillsides,
flocking to the black branches of the trees.
They deaden the air with their nevermore calls.
They sweep up and around and across
in the cold, winter wind,
calling and complaining,
thickening the air with their black bodies.
Acres of whirling crows!
The air a hundred feet deep in crows!
Cold! cold! they cry,
nervous and abandoned,
scraps of cinder,
flying rags,
whirling arm bands.

Song of the Bullet

Such a small thing!
to be so common and so deadly.
Such a small thing
to take so large a thing as my friend's life.
The little leaden egg
in its nest of brass.
It hatches so quickly
and learns so much in only one lesson!
It is born with a click and a thunder.
It fluffs out its smoky wings
and takes its only flight,
and spins so straight and true
(no straighter thing do we know)
straight into the heart
and muscle
and lung
of our brother.

Song of Insanity

It was the poison in the air.
At night, under my door,
it leaked into my room.
It snaked across my floor,
up the posts of my bed,
and into my ear.
A worm at the corner of my brain
an itch at the base of my skull.
A voice calling—
I don't know what it was calling
or why it called me.
But always. Always.
No smell,
no sign,
not even a drift of smoke.
But still, I knew,
it was a poison in the air,
pouring into my room
and down the funnel of my ear.

Because

Because the comfort of one is the poverty of another.
Because god left the job undone
Because there is no escape from pain
Because it was all a lie
Because Jesus himself went homeless and unemployed
Because property is theft
Because no one else would
Because it said so in the Bible
Because of the arrows of conscience
Because there is no peace
Because he believed what they told him
Because there is no justice
Because the cold winter wind is called the hawk;
      it whispers down the alleys
      it sweeps through the parks with a killing whisper
Because it is all a mystery
Because nothing else will save us
Because the sultans of culture despise the poor
Because the heart is the center of all true wealth
Because a person only needs just a little to live
Because life is hard
Because the world is sad
Because the Pharisees are reborn more often than Jesus
      and the money-changers plan to redevelop the temple
Because the widow's mite is remanded to Dives and Herod
Because City Council passed an ordinance to outlaw gleaning
Because the heart is where god lives
Because there are just a few sure things
Because he wanted to be innocent
Because he would be governed by no law but one:
Therefore, he left his home
he took up his cross
and was nailed to the floor of his office.

The Song of Damage

There is no calling back a bullet.
The damage cannot be undone.
The hammer trips.
The bullet flies.
The nose of it touches the gate of the body
and opens it like a key.
Quickly, as if it had a plan—
no time for argument—
it pushes all aside.
Nothing stops it.
Nothing dares.
Its little head is bathed in blood and lymph
and whatever bile or juice is in its path.
Sweet or bitter,
the fluids stream back
like water from the head of a diver.
Everything crowds out of the way.
Muscles cringe; they bleed and whimper.
Lungs shiver and fail.
The glands, like sunstruck turtles,
blink and withdraw.
And the harried waitresses of the intestines!
They spill everything!
Some bullets pass all the way through the body:
a little door at the front,
a larger door at the back.
But some stop at a bone like a boat come to dock
or like a runner, exhausted,
who pants against a wall.

A Story of Ash

All that was left was a box of gray crumbs.
A little box
such as one might use for pencils
or to save old letters.
Such a small box to hold the remains of a man.
On the day of the funeral march,
they strapped the box to his bicycle
and it marched right with us
through the streets.
Then, after the speeches, prayers, and song,
there was a quiet time
when those who loved him most closely
took the box of ash
and spooned the granules of cinder
into the places he most favored,
the park, the alley, the garden,
and the yard of the homeless shelter.
And I imagine that,
among those who most closely loved him,
one had a thought
to place a pinch of cinder on her tongue.
For what a power that might give!
But ash is bitter.
I do not think she did so.
They scattered the ash
into the grass of each place,
and it drifted down to the hardened earth
to rest among the broken glass
dried blood
mole skulls
lost buttons
fragments of torn letters
the roots of the grass
and the hidden bones
of the uncasketed poor.

BOOK II

Raven of Truth / Raven of Memory

At dusk,
crows flock by pairs to the television towers,
bringing the news to the one-eyed god.
Grief! cries Memory. Grief!
Cold! cries Truth. Cold!
Mother! Alas, Mother! cries Memory.
Milk! and Warmth! and Safety!
Stone! cries Truth. Stone!
Home! cries Memory. Home!
Shelter! and old clocks!
Meals in the kitchen!
The embrace of all who love you!
Wind! cries Truth. The wind!
The wind is a terrible hawk
with an eye that misses nothing!
Father! cries Memory. Father!
Old shoes! The coins from Italy!
The stern lessons! The hammer!
Dust, whispers Truth. Dust.
Dust blown in at the doorway.

Song of the Cold

November is followed by
December is followed by
the aching new year
with its bone-split weather.
It rasps at the knuckles;
it crackles in the lungs.
The heart is a sieve;
when the wind cuts right,
the cold can slice through a man
as if he were a shadow.

The news here is always the same.
A million trees die for the daily papers.
The frozen homeless are stacked for cinderblocks.
Ten million women have mailed their ovaries to Congress
and are awaiting further instructions.
For fear of invasion,
every farm in the country has been disguised
as a strip mall or a subdivision.
The children of the South Bronx
have volunteered to fast one week each month
to help us balance the budget.
Business is Great.
Life is Wonderful.
And the shining Republic stands ever so tall.

Disgusted with it all,
I walk the streets in the mankilling cold.
My breath is one small white twist
of vapor in the wind.
The snow is thick on the park benches,
thick on the black branches of the trees.
The muffling snows kill all sound
but the call of the crows.

And if I stand in the center of the park,
and if I close my eyes,
you are there.
I feel you at my shoulder.
I sense the rise and fall of your chest.
A tuft of your hair blows across my face.

But I can only hear the cold call of the crows.

The Mob of Crows

Evening, and we stalk homeward through the woods.
We have just met, face to face,
silent,
with a herd of timid deer
and we are radiant with the news.
But as we come to the top of the hill,
we hear, in the thick leaves of the tallest trees,
a sound as if of animals mating,
or dying,
a strangled, desperate croak
that stretches into a howl
and a sound of thrashing leaves and branches.
We want to know, what is this struggle?
At fifty yards, we cannot see.
At thirty, twenty, still.
Finally: the gray horned castle of an owl
in siege by a mob of crows.
One dives in to peck at the owl's flank;
he raises a wing,
stretches out a claw,
and the crow veers back to his branch.
One more attack
and the owl tumbles to a lower branch.
Another attack, and he flaps up to a higher.
The growling crows give him no rest.
We want to know, why do they harass him?
My companion thinks they want to wear him down,
then they can kill him for a meal.
She shouts to the crows: Go away!
The owl is so fine an animal
and this is no fair fight.
She throws rocks and branches
that she finds on the ground.
But this battle is in the tallest trees
and she cannot reach.
The white, open sky flares with falling light.
The trees darken; our path is dissolving.
We will have to feel our way home.

These bandit crows should be roosting by now.
They should be gathering with the hundreds
on the blackening hillsides.
But, reckless of the hour and the light,
they peck, growl, flap, hop from limb to limb
in search of an unguarded moment to thrust a beak,
to break a wing, dislodge a claw.
We watch, from our plot of impotent ground
until it seems there is no hope.
And perhaps there is none.
We no longer see the night-colored crows
but we hear them growl and attack.
The owl is that graying patch among the black branches
and we think, surely, he is lost.
But we hear a last alarm among the crows.
They scatter and growl.
The owl spreads his wings out wide.
Suddenly, he is a totem,
brave and masterful.
He springs from the branch
and breaks for the open, unresolved sky,
sweeping the wind with wide oars.
Behind him trail the crows,
black rags
tied to the tail of a kite.

When My Mother Died

When my mother died,
my hand was on her shoulder.
She had suffered through
a year of tests and operations,
of pain and delirium.
By the end,
there was nothing left of her
but a little shell,
a thin cocoon
in which
a little heart steadily beat
and a little pair of lungs fluttered.
For days, she slept.
Her heart beat and her lungs worked and growled.
My father and I waited over magazines.
Suddenly,
her breathing grew stiff.
I heard a crackle of phlegm.
I sent my father to call a nurse.
He hesitated a moment and I felt guilty
but he went.
Her lung crackled three more times.
I placed my hand on her shoulder,
her cat-thin and wasted shoulder.
I felt her last breath—
a soft, exhausted cackle—
under my palm.
Oh, Mom
I called.
But my hand could not hold her.
It was as if she were escaping
down a long, long hallway.

And it was many years,
many years
before I could make her hear me again.

Song of Suddenness

I do not understand, my friend.
You left so quickly!
All in a thunder and a flash!
Quick as a curse!
Not even a full morning's work.
So many things left undone.
The city, just wakened,
stretches her muscles and looks around.
The downtown stores wait shuttered behind their iron grates.
The crows reconnoiter the hillsides.
In the factories, workers look to the clock;
still an hour to morning break.
In the coffee shop, the breakfast run is over;
the waitress clears the counter.
The sun warms the bones
that gather on the benches of the park.
The third shift worker
draws the blinds
and curses the neighbor's radio.
In school, children yawn over their pencils.
And the prostitute,
she is so sad,
the all-hour prostitute,
she stands in the slanting light
smiles
and throws her hip
at every car that passes.
All around,
computers begin to hum and glow.
If we could see them,
if we could strip away the walls,
they would make a constellation!
So much life!
Everything throbs, pulses, aches with life!
Some is good; some is bad.
It does not matter.
Birth, joy, pain, struggle,
perhaps more joy, perhaps more sorrow,
it does not matter, we want to cling to it.

Bitter or sweet, we want it on our tongue.
But off we go, there is no argument.
We go. We go so quickly.
Burdened with curses
or armed with blessings,
we suit up and join the long march.
We leave behind
all that we curse
and all that we bless:
the crackhead's dry cough
the cry of children in the street
the air spiraling into our lungs
the drumbeat of our hearts
the old tired story of greed
the caress of all who love us

As the Crow Flies

Straight
through the mists of morning
he rises,
leaving the branch of pine where he has waited.
He crosses the eroding field of corn,
the irrigation ditch,
and the pale road of gravel,
and sets his course,
straight,
over the water tower and the village hall.
Field after field, he flaps over
broad rectangles of soybeans
then the smaller rectangles
of the swelling suburbs.
He crosses the malls and golf courses,
places barren as a sea of plastic,
and does not look down.
He crosses the black ring of the beltway
choked with tractor trailers
and the parkway
planted thick with SUVs.
To his right and to his left pass
the towers of the cell phones
the radio stations
and the star-headed towers of the television.
He slides an updraft over the factories
humming and yawning with the start of the shift
and the dark somnolent mills
still sleeping under a blanket of dust and abandonment.
The morning light blazes at the flanks
of the corporate centers in their pools of chilled asphalt.
But he does not look to the right or the left,
nor does he veer to either side.

He flies steady and true,
straight
across the apartment complexes
straight
down the lanes of the tormented projects
straight
to the throbbing center
straight
to the pierced heart of the city.

Blackness of the Crow

No blacker thing living
Blacker than night
Black to the beak
Black at the eye
Black at the claw
Black in the dark of the gullet
Black in the small black trap of the brain
No gloss
No shade
Radiant blackness
A page torn out of the visual
The veil ripped back
Scrap of otherworld in the shape of a bird

Four Songs of Silence

1

Why did my voice catch in my throat?
For forty days,
each time I tried to speak of you,
I had not words, but sand.
My throat thickened.
I grew hoarse.
A dove exploded in my chest.
So many others were speaking.
Why did I fall to such a silence?

2

There is a silence of ash.
There is a silence of moulder.
There is a silence of the tricking of seed from the beard of wheat.
A silence of daily fear.
A silence of the room where one will not be forgiven.
A silence of abandoned houses, uncurtained windows,
         a garden gone thick with nettles.
A silence of stone.
A silence of a field of grass.
A silence of too many hours riding the bus.
A silence of four o'clock in the morning.
A silence of three people in the room
         and each looks out a separate window.
A silence of sex—one talks, but only at a whisper.
A silence at the edge of the sea.
A silence of grief.

3
After all the hours of argument
After the seven speakers
After the commissions
After the words of love
After the scree of the nighthawks
After the strategy sessions
After the scuttle of rats in the alley
After the songs
After the blueprints, the audits, the manuals of policy
After the ordering of sandwiches
After the calculation of budgets
After the phone calls, the endless phone calls
After the chants on the picket lines
After the testimonies
After the shouts of children in the street:
The explosions
      five piercing explosions,
      five cruel explosions
      that tore out the heart of the morning.
Now,
such a silence, my friend.
Silence of a cold white room.

4
I fall easily to silence.
Even when I speak,
my words, piped thinly,
are ever flagged with sadness.
Even when I laugh,
even when I sing,
even when I talk of love,
I hear the note of a slender pipe.

Shadow sound.

A crow's black line across the sun.

Six Short Songs of Smoke

Gray exhalation
Breath of the oven.

A string of rags in air.
Tail of a kite of ash.

A woman, tall and slender:
Feet of flame
Long black dress
She hides her face
Her long fine hair streams away in the wind.

We all burn,
some slowly, some quickly.
In the earth, or in the flame.

This man had been all on fire all his life.
And now,
a little column of soot and gas.

Seven crows lift from a field as one.
They reach the ladders of the air
and disperse.

The Corpse of the Crow

This bird must have borne his body lightly,
for he weighs no more in my hands
than a cupful of ash,
no more than a husk,
no more than my mother when she died,
no more than a snatch of breath.
I have no fear of him now,
beak or claw;
he does not growl at me,
nor glare with his bright black eye,
nor stump in a wounded circle,
single-winged,
more fearful of me
than of the trucks of Eastern Avenue.
Yet I hold him gingerly,
so light in my hands,
I feel he might float off,
and with respect,
as if he were a chalice
(though I know this is from guilt
for I could not save him.
Clumsy, fearful,
I know I made his dying harder).
Now, I admire him closely
in his undiluted blackness.
For there is, I think,
nothing blacker than the blackness
of this tar-drop eye
that glints with bright liquid light.
And there is nothing blacker
than the blackness of these feathers.
Each barbule is alive
with stark, black light:

the mail of the breast,
the broad black oars of the wings,
the curtains of the throat,
the tufted crest at the peak of the skull,
the quilted layers that blanket the legs,
and the small, intricate feathers that guard the eye,
matted by what seems to be
a single black tear.
And I admire the perfect machinery of the beak,
milled and crafted
with the clean lines of a chisel.
And the black-greaved, leathered legs,
jointed like a crustacean
and fitted with mechanical claws.
I fold him, carefully,
into bullet shape
and place him, for burial,
in the crotch of a tree.
Broken ark
Bird of warning
Temple of cinders
Casket of the lost voice.

BOOK III

Awakening

Two crows awaken in the snow at dawn.
All night, they have roosted
on an iron truss of the television tower.
All night, the red light at the peak of the tower
pulsed in their dream
like a bolus of radiant blood.
Now, they shake the snow from their shoulders
and stretch their wings and legs.
They are cold at the claw,
cold in the joints.
Snow stretches all around them,
caked in the branches of the trees,
along the power lines,
and in the untracked street.
They call, they call
to warm themselves,
then lift from the iron roost
to feel the cold air under their wings.
The city roars with traffic.
The cables hum with messages.
Even the trusses of the tower
thrum with an electric mumble.
But other birds hear the call of the birds
and they answer.
Soon the hillside rattles
with the gravel of their voices.
Up in the crow-patterned air
they call again and call again.
They greet and they are greeted.

The Weighted Hour

There is an hour
when the world is too weighted for us to bear.
When the minutes press on us
like the stones of Salem.
An hour when the slant light falls to ash.
When the red-eyed liar gnaws at the ear.
When there is no end to the drone of engines
and no end to the sad parades.
An hour when anger clots the lungs.
When there is no hope.
Then I look to the lonely crow.
There, in his cold rooms
high above the red tips of the maples
above the strung wires
above the cell phone towers
he is a black ship in a vast bottle.
He works his wings in short bursts against the wind
then coasts for a time,
works in a burst, then coasts again.
Then I want to think myself the crow,
eagling across a broken heartland.
Far below me,
the asphalt ribbons and bulldozer scars.
Far below me,
the suburban checkerboard.
Far below me,
the gash of abandoned factories.
Far below me,
rivers that choke with the runoff of the poisoned farms.
Far below me,
small men walk green fields hitting small white balls.
Far below me,
strip malls, theme parks.
Far below me,
the broad, separate roofs of houses
        on streets that meander like the tunnels of the mole.

Far below me,
the close-packed roofs of the projects.
And I am sad,
for I see nothing that looks like home.
The horizon is wide.
And far off,
at the line where the red sun sets,
I see the gray fences
and the leaning stalks of corn.
The light leans to the earth's back door.
I search the dusk
for my brothers
and my sisters.
I call them
in a voice
of husks
and gravel.

Nightfall

Nightfall,
and the cold crows rally
in the hillside trees.
At my feet,
the sod canopies of the mole
are crisp with frost.
They crumble at my step.
At such an hour,
I feel the weight of the stone-ribbed world
and I think that life is hard.
But every evening
these birds gather
to story one another
with their calls.
And the mole lies tight
in his deepest chamber.

A Trapped Voice

You died, my friend,
and my voice was a crow caught under a net.
I could not lift the wings of speech.
The world turned suddenly;
the wind of it withered the stalk of my throat
and picked the pockets of my lungs.
There is no accounting for such things.
I have no reason for it.
I only know my words were trapped
like a bird with weighted wings.

Song of Wounds

I look at you, my friend,
and I see nothing but wounds.
Just one wound,
and you might still be with us.
We might tell stories,
we might embrace as brothers.
But no,
there are far too many wounds.
The blood,
broken from its familiar channels,
is naked and confused.
Muscles, unstrung, will not stand.
Nerves throw up their pale hands in surrender,
for there are just too many wounds.
I press my fingers to the lips of each.
I note the contours closely.
I see them in their intimate and parasitical relations.
I give each one a name:
the one that tore at the moorings of the lungs
the one that cut at the roots of the liver
the one that frayed the ropes of the intestines
the one that broke through bone like an axe
the one that shattered the beating heart.
Yes, today, I see nothing but wounds.
Wounds in the alley
Wounds in the park
Wounds blackened in the asphalt of the beltway
Wounds with the marks of the teeth of the wind
Wounds in the bellies of small brown children.
Wounds sleepless at four in the morning
Wounds in the disordered ladders of the cell:
Five wounds,
and I ponder over them within me.
Five wounds, sharp as a hammer
Five wounds in the shock of morning
Five wounds and there is no escape
Five wounds, five curses
My friend!
My friend!
I see nothing today but wounds!

Washington Park, Cincinnati, Ohio

This park was built upon a Potter's Field.
Heaped, indiscriminate, and abandoned,
the bones of the poor form its joists and pillars.
They were killed in another century
by a forgotten epidemic and
the untreatable virus of poverty.
Barbers, prostitutes, painters, domestics,
mechanics, teamsters, bakers, seamstresses—
all these, and their spindling children who even
at their best had teetered over a tiny grave—
all were shoved in here by threes and dozens.
No stone or marker now gives us their names
or tells us how they are enearthed among the
monuments and benches and the shading
oaks and maples. I think of them each time
I walk this ground. I think of how they lie
unrecognized, bereft, anonymous,
though I do not think they care. The dead are wise.
They do not look for praise or tombstones.
The park is sad in this bare-branched blackening
season, when frost tips each naked twig of
the leaf-torn maples. By day, the homeless
in their hand-out coats wait on the benches
for meal-time and a pallet on the floor
and crows pick over wasted chips and bits
of sandwich. Children play on the cannon.
And traffic flows around this green island.
By night, the floodlights glancing off the face
of Music Hall drive moon-like shadows down
among the mottled sycamores and down
onto the mottled faces of the men
asleep and cold on benches, and the crows
aroost on narrow, wind-shaken branches.
The night is long in such a season
and there are varied worrisome dangers
for the unsheltered. So I think the dead
patrol each frost-edged night; they climb the ladders

of the roots and watch among the benches and
the trees. They watch the shuddering homeless in
their cold and fearsome sleep. They even watch
the concert-goers as they hustle past
into the safety of the lighted stairs.
They watch the couple making desperate love
beneath the bushes near the cannon. They watch
the cold rookeries of the crows. For they have joined
the Great Commune; they know their duties to
the living; and I am grateful for them
though they cannot do a thing to save us.
The night is long in any season and
I think it is a comfort that they watch
with us, to know that they will keep watch until
the light of morning tingles at the black
crow-heavy branches and the men yawn out
their stiffened muscles, the lovers shiver
one more time together and the cold crows
stretch out their feathers, shake out the black frost
and find their harsh and raucous morning voices.

The Chambers of the Mole

The dark chambers of the mole
extend for yards and yards
beneath a roof of grass.
Walls of clay.
Walls of sand.
Walls of warming compost.
Pantry stocked with earthworms
and the pale, larval locusts.
I imagine him lonely in his mansion;
he roams from room to room,
parting the curtains of the roots,
misering over bits of clothing
a long white bone
shards of china
spent bullet casings
pull tabs from aluminum cans
and pages from old letters
torn small
the ink
blurred by the damp.
He turns these over,
these corroding archeological knickknacks,
one by one
in his big pink hands.
Above him,
visible only in the broken seams of sod,
snap banners of bright light.

Song of Drought

The park is weighted
with the sagging bodies of the homeless.
Trees bend under the heat.
The leaves are brass.
Bark splits like the shell of a locust.
The paths that lead from corner to corner
go black; the dust is the color of cinder.
No cloud, no hope of rain.
I want to know:
Will there be an end to this season of dust?

That Day

In the moment he died
nothing stopped.
The world continued rolling toward dark
and the dark continued rolling toward day.
In grocery stores, shoppers filled their carts.
Some mounded their carts high.
Some barely mounded them at all.
The moles of the park
raised up the grass
on their small shoulders
in search of grubs and worms.
The sirens wailed above them
but they did not hear.
In the bar on the corner,
a third shift man
just in for his shot and a beer
wiped the foam from his mustache
with the back of his hand
and headed home to a dreamless sleep.
On the Shopping Channel
there was much excited talk
of zircons and vacuum cleaners
at attractive prices.
On Wall Street,
trading opened
and the Dow began its daily march.
And somewhere,
perhaps in Bangkok,
a girl,
just brought in from the country
on the back of a truck,
is tired.
They have given her something strange to eat
and her mind feels so very strange.
She is pushed into a room with a naked man
and the door is locked.

And somewhere,
a boy is handed his very first gun.
And somewhere,
a nun is strangled.
All these things went on.
The stones of the earth continued to grind.
School bells rang on schedule.
Fires were lit under steam tables.
Trucks rolled into weigh stations.
Commuters pressed into the doors of a subway.
A child looked out the classroom window
        past the playground
        past the fence
        past the suburban rooftops
        past the cell phone towers.
In our little city,
editorialists
stacked their words
and sharpened their knives.
And the stars
continued
their subtle realignment
of this galaxy
and the next
and the one beyond.

The Hunger of the Dead

This is what I do not like about the dead:
That they are so hungry.
They are so lonely and demanding.
Remorseless, with their earthen mouths,
we feel them grazing at our necks.
And there is no escape from them;
we are utterly outnumbered.
We cannot hide; they find us anywhere.
I do not understand the hunger of the dead,
nor why the living feed them.
But still they draft us to their sad army.
Still they lead us on the endless march
and will not say where we are going.
And I did love my mother;
I did not want to see her leave.
But when she did,
it was as if she took my hand,
as when I was a child,
and started me down the long passage
where I did not want to travel
and pushed me toward a light
I did not want to see.

The Work of the Dead

In every life cut short,
so many things are left undone.
The dishes stacked and crusting in the sink.
The dogs unfed.
Three new strings on the guitar,
the others still in their wrappers.
The bedroom half-painted,
one side fresh and glossy,
the other a map of patching plaster islands.
And the oil that really ought to be changed.
And the letter unsent:
it only needs a stamp
and someone to walk it to the mailbox.
And all the work of love:
words and gestures
still bundled
in their little proud houses
and the keys
lay right on the table where we left them.
And even the nation,
this sprawling, addled nation:
Such a tangle of dropped threads,
interrupted projects,
failed promises.
Who will beat down the hammers of greed?
Who will untangle the knots of deceit?
Those whose lives have been cut short
are crowded into their darkened theater
where they watch us
bawling and arguing
like actors in an ancient drama.
They watch us closely,
for they want to know
who will take on
the unfinished work of the dead.

BOOK IV

The Tower Will Not Answer

Two birds strut among the leaves of the park.
They turn over twigs, fragments of paper,
and watch for any little scrap, a word,
a story, any little fragment that
will make a seeming sense out of this scene.
At dusk, they fly to the hillside tower.
> What can I tell you? A man is dead and
> at the hand of one he loved and cared for.
> His friends are torn. His mother weeps. And now?
> What of the man who drove the leaden nails?
Madness! One caught in the talons of madness!
> He sits in a cell and curses; he begs
> the state to crush him. Then curses again.
A life of curses. Cursed from birth. Wounded
at the stem; the wound, unhealed, bled curses.
> He paces his cell and curses. He knows
> no one. His curses ring against the stone
> of walls, against the iron doors; they muffle
> within the glass of the watchroom of the guards.
He has never known aught but a curse.
Even a blessing, to his poisoned ear,
has the sound, the suspect feel, of a curse.
> He has two cells; the one of stone and glass,
> and one whose walls now press the aching brain
> from every side.
> > Remorse! Remorse! Remorse!
Wind closes on the door of day. The birds
look up to the mute red eye at the peak
of the tower. They call, and call, and call.
The red eye blinks, is silent, blinks, and blinks.
The birds grip tight on the strut of the tower
They shudder out their feathers for the warmth
that shuddering might give. They shut their onyx eyes.
And sleep.

A Woman Cursing

I see a woman cursing in the street.
She has thrust herself into the crush of traffic
and a car, to miss her, must cross lanes.
The driver, wary, shrinks under her heat
but she ignores him; she has other fish to fry.
She curses loudly and without shame
and the young men of the sidewalk turn to watch her.
The prostitute eyes her from her corner perch.
A clerk worries from the window of the Jordan Market
and, in the schoolyard, a nun folds her arms and stares.
Perhaps she mumbles a prayer for the woman
who is large; she ripples with anger.
I cannot hear her curses
but they buzz against the glass of my car.
I cannot see the target of her curses,
but I see the hand she points
and the firm set of her foot.
I see the narrowed wince of her eyes
and the path of the curses down her tongue and off her lips
and into the street and into the solemn ears of children.
I see the roped muscles tighten at her neck
and the twine of the nerves beneath her hatchmark brows.
And I am sad to see her so.
Sad that the world can be so raw.
Sad that the air of the street has filled with poison.
Sad that the masters of television mock her poverty.
Sad that the honey is leaving the combs of the earth.
Sad that the milk of the world is tainted with salt.
Sad that this path is cluttered with stones.
Sad that there is so much pain—
     You, me, and this woman on the street.
Ah, God, I cannot lift such sadness!

Prostitute at Walnut and Liberty

She stands her corner,
squares her shoulders,
and scans the streets
with a professional, fire-hardened eye.
There is much for her to watch.
Cars nurse at the pumps of the Shell station.
Carpenters glance back at her as they shoulder their lumber.
Dope boys, arrogant shadows on the opposite corner,
study the noonday traffic.
And so does she.
A BMW passes an aging Toyota,
a patrol car spreads blue light
across an Audi with tinted windows,
and a pickup truck stops short,
cut off by an SUV
the size of a small Midwestern town.
And on it goes.
Impatient,
she strides one way,
then another.
Some cars cruise slowly round her corner
and the men who drive the cars
turn their eyes from the traffic to gaze at her.
She stares them back
with a question in her brow
and sometimes a word
and sometimes a shift of her shoebox hips.
(She has gone, you see, so very slim.
She has that hollow in the jaw;
she has that shadow below each eye.)
I do not know what these men see when they see her
but I know
she has a golden brain
and a rapid heart
and internal organs shapely as fruit
and silver nerves
that have been frailed and fouled by crack cocaine.

And I know that
when she was small
she was greeted with joy
and she was greeted with dismay
and when she cried she was comforted
and when she cried she was ignored
and she was fed and coddled
and she was not-fed and she was cursed
and her life which was perfectly normal
and her history which was utterly cruel
have brought her to this corner
where she studies the passing cars
and the glances of the men in the cars.
She sweeps the street with a hungry eye
and she is not satisfied.
She strides one way, then another,
down one street and back.
Her arms swing like hammers
but she always comes back
to her post on the corner
where, quickly, she looks right, she looks left,
then right and left again,
like a hawk on a rail.

Song of Anger against the Lie

I do not like a lie, not one.
Not even my own, most protective lie.
Not even the lie that shelters what I most want hidden.
Not even the lie that bandages a wound.
But who can live without a lie?
It seems too much to bare our naked selves
without the dressing of prevarication.
The sleet world chills us quickly
if we cannot wrap ourselves in walls and glass—
the many little lies we use, like nails,
to tack in place a shelter for the self,
and which are merely sad.
But other lies are fierce; they raise up fear and rage.
Lies for theft and massing dollars.
Lies that dress us in hatred.
Cattle-prod lies that teach the soul to cower.
Lies designed to do what the fist cannot.
These are lies most terrible.
But I fear most
the blind, cruel lies of politicians.
Word, by word, the politician's lie hems in the poor
from left and right.
Told long enough and well,
a single lie can raze a village.
Broadcast lies, spread by the nets of television,
fill quickly with air and mount the skies of policy.
In Washington, in every statehouse,
they hold hands with their think-tank brothers.
Quick and confident, in their crisp black suits,
lies stride the marble corridors.
They always take express, no need to trudge the stairs,
and glide to the peak of the tallest of towers
to beam out proposals and projects and status reports.
Into the neighborhoods, the suburbs, the farm country.
The lie, airborne, slips over every transom and under every door.

It hides in the closets of the cell
to infect us with madness and the will to condemn.

Ah, the glossy, go-everywhere electron lie!

What does he care about the little weed of truth?

Things which Are Small

Things which are small
can indeed confound the mighty.
But mostly, they must dodge the large.
The mole
The grub
The caddis nymph that scuttles in the gravel of a stream.
They live as targets.
The trout sips the caddis.
The crow spikes the grub.
The mole stumbles into the suburban guillotine.
Their little lives are always in danger.
They have no insurance.
The merest accident wrecks everything.
Consider the ants,
hidden in the alleys of the grass.
Stressed-out engineers
working without blueprints in the dark,
busy and futile, on permanent overtime,
erecting their caverns and complexes, their little dark malls,
the whole village doing daycare
and staffing the cafeteria.
the only thing we see is that cone of dirt on top.
But below are the blind factories
running all three shifts.
All it takes is the scuff of an ignorant shoe,
the step of a hoof,
the beat of a paw,
and the whole project crushes inward.
Alarms go off.
Everybody rushes for the exits.
The ceilings come down acrumble
around their antennae.
All systems are disrupted.
Dozens suffocate, others are cut off.
All the elements of catastrophe.
The shoe, the hoof, the paw moves on.
Now what do they do?
Their nervous systems are much too small and simple for grief.
Each cranium is no bigger than a moment
and cannot hold another moment but this.

They cannot know loss as we know loss.
They form no committees,
hold no funerals,
frame no elegies.
They do not petition for disaster relief.
No time! No time for that!
They schedule no memorials,
say no prayers.
Grain by grain,
they begin to dig and drill.
Brainlessly, they rebuild.

A Song of Wind

A cold night when the wind pulls down the stars.
We keep watch in our kitchen and hear
the wind rattle the black branches of the trees.
It sets loose shingles; they sail
across the yard like black-winged birds.
It flaps out the jackets of old magazines
and they prattle down the street.
It snows the petals from the cherry tree in the park
and bangs the trash cans over the sidewalks.
I think of the crows
bobbing and huddled on their narrow perches
and of the deer in their stands of willow
and of the refugee
who staggers across the spine of a Balkan mountain
and of the homeless
pressed into doorways
or tunneled in the deepest chambers of the alleys,
each of them pierced by the wind as by a nail.
The wind does not invade the dark rooms of the mole
with his walls of earth
or his ceiling of grass.
He digs and snuffles in the dark
and the wind is no more to him
than a rumor.
He hears it as one, well-insulated,
might hear a fight in the street,
or a noise of traffic,
or a distant war.
But all other things of flesh
shrink under the cut of the wind.
They hunker down,
search out holes for hiding.
Possum-still, they move so little,
we would think them stones.
We listen in our kitchen, barely moving,
and hope ourselves safe.
But the Serbian wind mocks us.

It searches out each crack and seam.
It whistles in the chimney like a great, clay pipe.
It presses against each pane of glass
to tell us, how thin are these walls,
how near we are to naked.

Crow in the Wind

The big wind rocks the hillside trees
like the arms of grief.
High above the rooftops
and the radio pylons
a single black bird
beats, beats against the wind
to stay in place.
I cannot fathom this bird's mission,
this cold pilgrim,
but he hangs in the gunsmoke sky
as if raised upon a cross.
The big wind draws down
the snows of Canada.
I want to be
in the silence of the dark trees.
I want to be
where the wind rushes through
the fingers of the dark trees.

Funeral March

A day of bright and bitter cold.
Silent, we march the stony blocks and hear
only the tread of feet on the pavement
thousands of feet on the stony pavement,
only the banners that billow, snap,
and bellow out again.
Only these,
and the snap of the drum.

We enter the park
watched by bullet-colored crows,
silent and alert.

We pass the stone gates; the drum stops.
Song overlaps the silence.
Singing, we fill this small place
with our small hundreds.
We tread the ground that was once a Potter's Field.
The earth beneath us is riddled with bones.
From their dark porches, the dead observe us
through a screen of grass.

From the band shell there are speeches, more song.
Around the band shell, handshakes and embraces.
My small son and I sit close and listen.
I ask him, are you cold? he denies it.
But he shivers, so I lend him my coat.
His arms are lost within the sleeves;
the hem devours his knees.
He is a little, shivering thimble,
a haystack nipped at the ears.
But he does not complain.
He has marched each cold and stony step.
Now, he follows each word of the speeches.
He sings each song, chants each chant.

We are watched, in our small hundreds,
under the bright, over-shouldering cloak of the sky,
by the cycloptic eye of television,
by the shivering homeless at the edges of the park,
by the cold, curious crows in their balcony seats among the trees,
by the investors in carrion, sniffing the air for a hint of decay,
and by the dead, standing at attention in their dark ranks.
And so we are not alone.
A hyena greed beats and pants around us
in all its stink and pretension
all its need and triviality,
shivering with poison,
shedding pain and madness.
And I want to tell myself
we are much too small.
But I have been too long in despair.
(I have not ever said it, but there it is, despair!)
I have laid in it like a prisoner
whose appeals have been long denied.
And I am ready for this clean and bitter cold.
My son, who shivers in my coat,
is too small a boy
to wear such great things as I want for him.
But when I see his grave, intelligent eye
and his cheeks pinched bright by the cold
I recall to myself
the duty of hope.

BOOK V

Voice of the Crows

Crows in the tree line at dusk,
tucked among thick leaves and the curtains of pine.
Ghost birds: I cannot see them,
but I hear them call, call in their raw, insistent voices.
Each crow I hear has his own particular call,
her own unmatched voice.
They growl, bark, chatter, purr.
They pitch high or pitch low.
They scrawk long like a knife on a stone
or pierce, sudden and sharp.
One call is sand, another gravel.
And there is one, fescue-thin,
whose copper voice reminds me of my own.
What do they call, one to another?
I do not understand this language of hammers and scratches.
They are long past mating season
and they do not seem to argue.
What is it they must say each night
in their rooking in the hillsides?
Only this: *I'm here! I'm here!*
I have outlived the dangers of the day
I'm here! I'm here!
And in the morning,
I'm going! I'm going!
We meet again at nightfall!
I'm gone! I'm gone!

A Blessing

This man wears dark clothes and is,
in fact, a dark, dark man.
I see him often on the labyrinth streets.
Always in the same black clothes
shirt, sweater, jacket
and a long, black overcoat that reaches to his knees.
These are piled, layer on layer
dark on dark
as if he had been lacquered.
And the eyes so wide!
and the brows so wide and startled!
And the dredlocks to the shoulders,
a frozen waterfall of intricate hair.
He is multi-layered and mysterious as a rare onion.
Day by day,
I see him mumble to himself,
or count verses
one by one
down the pages of a leatherback bible.
Sometimes I see him stand
crucified to the cold air,
nailed palms and feet
by the cold hammers of winter.
Holding vigil in the street,
he could be a crow in a mid-winter field.
Dark, against the bustle and fog
at the windows of the laundromat
Dark against the press of buyers and sellers at the market
Dark against the leaning, sad prostitute
Dark against the dope boys in their bright coats
with the gold at their necks.

Dark as a scrap of night
blown into the street from yesterday's news.
Dark as a congress of crows.
Dark as Mister Death.
And I think he tells me not to fear such a dark.
For today, I see him and he is, again,
so like a crow in a mid-winter field
for his hands, folded to pray,
are in the shape of a beak
and he pivots at the hip like a crow
who pikes at a kernel
or a bright silver grub.
Again and again he bows
before the ark of a broken covenant
swaying like a censer in the tabernacle streets.
He bows to the four corners
to the traffic
to the prostitute
to the dope boys
to the women folding laundry
behind the curtain of fog.
I slow to pass him and I raise my hand.
He smiles
with a smile of crucified ecstasy
and bows toward me also.
Suddenly, blessedly, I am in his crazy prayer.

The Study of Language

I have struggled to learn the language
of things which escape the scan of television
and the mockery of talk radio.
A language of grass and scrap metal,
a language of wood and nails.
A language of cheap wine and day-old bread,
of second-hand coats,
of leaves gathered along a fenceline.
A language in the crow's growl and gravel
and in the final bark of the mole.
A language in the clatter of the leaves of corn.
A language of lost letters, broken glass,
a photograph, cracked and faded,
pressed into the pages of a book.

Making a Voice

The crow pecks at hard seeds
and lines his throat with gravel,
the better to soften the corn,
and the better to make a voice,
for his call has a rasp
as of stone grinding on stone
or a knife he sharpens at a wheel.

Song of Virtues

For many years
I have studied the mute virtues of the mole.
Silence, persistence, humility,
digging, digging, digging.
Now I want the gifts of the crow,
the cunning, live-anywhere, communal crow
with the wings that lift him him above the asphalt
and the voice that cuts across a field
like a trumpet of stone.

The Day

On the day we first broke the air with a cry, it was love that called us out.
That day, a great force pushed us into a babel of voices.
The cold air snapped open our lungs,
the blade of light pierced our eyes,
and we shivered with the emptiness of our surroundings.
But it was love that called us
from the cell of warmth and blood
out from the prison of bone,
and into the clatter and embrace of the world.

On the day we quailed in the shadow of destruction,
it was love who spoke us courage.
That day (it was so many days)
we learned that the world had teeth and sting,
that we could see nothing behind us and only a little before.
To hide, we would shrink ourselves small as thought.
But it was love that called us
out of our habit of hiding,
out from the palisades of our own skin
and into the snarl and blessing of the world.

And in the days we labored at the tables of pride,
it was love who humbled us.
That day (so many days) we were oxen
hung with a yoke of our own making
and we trod the arrogant furrows
we had dug the year before.
It was love that wedged us out
from the grinding, millstone labor
out from the blind caves of self
and into the honey and thistle of the world.

And one day, there will be a day (just one day)
when we are crossed by five swift crows.
That day, the roads will end in a sea of silent grass,
and the breath we borrowed will come due.
We blink, the light is canceled, as if we had not paid the bill,
and the warm earth draws over us like a sheet.
It is sad, to leave such richness and grief,
but it was love that called us out,
and I think it is love who calls us back,
into the earthen lap and wintering birth of the world.

What the Dead Tell Us

I want to know
what might the dead tell us
if we know how to hear them?
I have listened in the pages of old letters
in the dust of cellars
and in the grip of tools.
I have listened in the chattering leaves of corn.
I have listened in the call of crows
and in the humped tunnels of the mole.
And I know the sayings of each of these by heart.
Now, I press my ear to the earth,
and hear
a sound of drumming,
voices
as if in chant
and a sound—
scuff-and-shuffle
scuff-and-shuffle—
as if of many feet
as if
in the halls of the dead
all are dancing.

A Teaching

I have been so often mute
when I wanted most to have you hear me.
But I have studied speech
with the mole and the crow
and the unsilent dead
who speak to us daily
with their mouths of clay
and their tongues of grass,
as they drill us in the old and necessary lessons.
And what do they teach?
I have no trick for telling you
all of what I think they say,
but I believe it comes to this:
There is no law
but that of love.
That takes courage
and we often fail.
Because we fail
forgiveness is basic as bread.
We fail there too.
And so the world is sad.
If I could have the voice I wanted once,
I would be your bard.
I would bind you to me
with firelight tales
of struggle and discovery
that would drive back your darkness for an hour.
But I have only this small voice
with which my father voiced me
a voice with the reed and rasp of the crow.
And I fear it is much too small.
Even so,
I tell you
There is no law
but the law of love.
Take courage.
Take courage.

After a Dark Season

So now, the winter rains have done.
In the park, and on the hillside,
buds force out their chalice-light leaves.
The grass, flag and parable of the dead,
crowds up and into every marble chink.
The mole humps and groans;
he thrusts up his sod chapels.
And in the tabernacle of an empty building
men stretch, grasp their heads,
and think of bread and wine.
This is the season of sacrifice and resurrection.
I cannot help but think of you my friend.
Your death, at the thunder of nine in the morning,
closed on my heart like a stone upon a tomb.
I lay beneath it, blind and mute,
for three days
and three days
and many days more.
Still nothing lifted.
But now, the winter rains have done;
so is this season of despair.
The rain of dollars falls steadily,
for it knows no season.
And the liar is at home with his lie.
The earth is paved with asphalt
and cluttered with subdivisions.
The armies of children march
with their god-sized guns.
And a man—he is riven by madness—
mutters and stalks in a room he will never leave.
The world is wrong beyond reason.
But I think you knew
that is not the only story we can tell.

The world shudders with a great work of redemption
and I am done with this season of despair.
The knife of Abraham cuts the boy away from the stone
and the ram of sacrifice struggles in the brush.
We are in the gears of something great and fine
and there is no reason for despair.
You know and I know, there is much to do
but we labor by Lazarus-light
with a blind, improbable joy.